HAUNTED HERITAGE

JOHN MASON

COLLINS & BROWN

First published in Great Britain in 1999
by Collins & Brown Ltd
64 Brewery Road
London N7 9NT

A member of **Chrysalis** Books plc

3 5 7 9 8 6 4 2

British Library Cataloguing-in-Publication Data:
A catalogue record for this book is available from the British Library.

ISBN 185585 693 X

Conceived, edited and designed by Collins & Brown

Editorial Director: Sarah Hoggett
Editor: Claire Waite
Designer: Claire Graham

Reproduction in Singapore by HBM Print Pte Ltd.
Printed and bound in Hong Kong by Imago

Cover: Thornton Abbey, Back cover: Warkworth Castle, Title page: Sutton Scarsdale Hall

HAUNTED HERITAGE

CONTENTS

Lindisfarne Priory

Dunstanburgh Castle

Warkworth Castle
TynemouthPriory
Hylton Priory

Carlisle Castle

DURHAM

Gisborough Priory

Castlerigg Stone Circle
Bowes Castle
Whitby Abbey
Richmond Castle
Rievaulx Abbey
Scarborough Castle
Byland Abbey
Pickering Castle
YORK
Spofforth Castle
Clifford's Tower
Skipsea Castle

LEEDS

Thornton Abbey
Conisbrough Castle
MANCHESTER
Roche Abbey
Gainsborough Old Hall
Peveril Castle
Nine Ladies Stone Circle
Bolsover Castle
Arbor Low Stone Circle
Sutton Scarsdale Hall
Rufford Abbey
Wingfield Manor

Binham Priory
Moreton Corbet Castle
Croxden Abbey
Castle Rising Castle
Burgh Castle

Haughmond Abbey
Lilleshall Abbey
Rushton Triangular Lodge
Thetford Warren Lodge

BIRMINGHAM
CAMBRIDGE
NORTHAMPTON

Arthur's Stone
Hailes Abbey
Rollright Stones
Goodrich Castle
Minster Lovell Hall
Rycote Chapel
Greyfriars & Blackfriars
OXFORD
Hadleigh Castle
LONDON
West Kennet Long Barrow & Avebury Stone Circle
Farnham Castle Keep
Reculver Tower & Roman Fort
BATH
Eynsford Castle
Richborough Castle
Farleigh Hungerford Castle
Waverley Abbey
Dover Castle
Stonehenge
Bayham Abbey

Old Wardour Castle
Bramber Castle
Battle Abbey
Sherborne Old Castle
Netley Abbey
Pevensey Castle
Okehampton Castle
Porchester Castle
BRIGHTON
Tintagel Castle
EXETER
Carisbrooke Castle
Appuldurcombe House
Lydford Castle
Berry Pomeroy Castle
PLYMOUTH

FOREWORD

ENGLISH HERITAGE HAS in its care over 400 historical properties, many of them dating from the very earliest periods of history, and some of them are still in use today. Many of these sites rouse strong echoes of the past and all have attached to them legends and mysteries which tell of the people who lived in them and the extraordinary events that happened there. These tales make the history of the sites come alive. For example, stone circles are maidens turned to stone for the sin of dancing on the Sabbath to music played by the Devil and Tintagel is seen as the legendary home of King Arthur. Inevitably, ghosts haunt the ruins too – grey ladies, headless drummer boys and World War II soldiers encountered in the tunnels beneath the cliffs at Dover Castle. These legends add to the fear – even dread – which is evoked in many of our visitors by the sheer age and grandeur of some of our ancient properties.

Much of the work we do consists of archaeological and architectural investigation, conservation and historical research. But we are nevertheless acutely aware that much of the appeal of our properties to visitors passes from the mere factual to the spiritual peace and tranquillity of abbeys like Rievaulx and Bayham, the evocation of battle that is evident at our ancient castles and the awesome mystery of 5000-year-old Stonehenge. It is this indefinable magic that we present in this book, captured by John Mason's marvellously evocative photographs of some of our more haunted sites, accompanied by some of the mysteries associated with them. You don't have to believe all these tales to shiver at the flickering glimpses they reveal of how men and women over the years lived and died leaving us their haunted heritage.

SIR JOCELYN STEVENS
CHAIRMAN, ENGLISH HERITAGE

LEFT *Dover Castle*

INTRODUCTION

ENGLAND'S GHOST STORIES date back to prehistoric times, many of them handed down through the centuries from generation to generation, and sites with ghostly associations have long exerted a fascination over our imaginations.

Ghosts are believed by many investigators of the paranormal to be the result of a traumatic event somehow imprinting itself on the landscape or into the very fabric of a site. If this is the case, then the ghost stories explored in this book – from the grieving Viking who wanders through Tynemouth Priory to the star-crossed lovers of Goodrich Castle swept to their deaths while fleeing the Civil War – may well hold the key to the most fascinating periods in a site's history. Far from being nonsensical fairy tales, they are as relevant to a site's history as any tangible remains and add extra interest for today's visitor. Archaeological finds and documentary evidence are vital to understand the past, but they tell only part of the story. England's heritage – its landscape and buildings – cannot be separated from the stories of the people who lived and died there.

English Heritage, the guardian of many of the country's most fascinating historic places, is dedicated to making the past come alive for the millions of people who flock to explore its sites each year. Their help in creating this photographic journey through the

LEFT *Waverley Abbey*

past has been invaluable. This project for English Heritage has taken me the best part of three years to complete and has been a labour of love. I have always been interested in England's heritage. As a child I loved visiting historic sites, especially if they were reputed to be haunted or had mysteries and legends attached to them. I don't however, regard myself as a 'ghost hunter', just someone who has a real love of old legends and taking photographs.

Nobody knows for certain if ghosts exist, but I like to keep an open mind on the subject. Think back to those times when you have felt a sudden chill on a warm summer's day or the time you caught a glimpse of a fleeting 'something' from the corner of your eye, or the feeling that someone or something is watching you; who knows what it could be?

I have visited many more properties than those that are included here. Those featured are some of the best, but England has so many more sites associated with myths and legends that are well worth exploring.

None of the pictures in this book have been altered or manipulated in the darkroom. Everything was shot using Canon EOS1N, with a 17–35mm lens, using Kodak black and white infrared film. The photographs were taken at various times of the day and in all seasons.

I hope you enjoy this book and I would love to hear from anyone who has had any 'ghostly' experiences.

JOHN MASON

RIGHT *Hailes Abbey*

THE
SOUTH EAST

O F ALL THE REGIONS OF ENGLAND, the South East has possibly the richest tradition of spectral visits and hauntings. For many years it has been a prime source of stories of ghostly sightings – sacrificed infants, starving children, missing brides, murdered Roman soldiers and monks are but a few of the phantoms who reportedly frequent the area's historical sights.

The stories range from the dramatic tales of blood running across the battlefield at Hastings to the tragic personal story of the new bride trapped in an attic while playing an innocent game with her husband at Minster Lovell Hall.

This region is known throughout the world for its ghostly goings-on, and the stories on the following pages show that this reputation is well deserved.

LEFT *Dover Castle*

Dover Castle

The current castle was constructed in the 12th and 13th centuries, and extensively redesigned in the 18th century, but fortifications have been on this site since prehistoric times. Beneath the castle are extensive underground tunnels which run for miles, some dating from the 13th century and others from the Napoleonic Wars. They were later used to mastermind the evacuation of Dunkirk during World War II.

Over the years the castle has been the subject of many accounts of hauntings. The ghost of a headless drummer boy murdered during the Napoleonic Wars has been seen, and staff have sighted phantoms in Royalist garb, as well as a lady in red and a figure in blue. A Roman soldier and a hooded monk are said to haunt the Roman 'pharos' or lighthouse, situated next to the Saxon church of St Mary-in-Castro.

The underground tunnels, formerly known as Hellfire Corner, have been the scene of several sightings of World War II personnel, to the extent that they have attracted the attention of paranormal research units who have carried out investigations.

The Rollright Stones

The Rollright Stones comprise three groups of
stones, known as 'The King's Men', 'The
Whispering Knights' and 'The King Stone'. They
date from the late Neolithic period, when,
legend tells us, a witch's curse turned an
invading Danish king and his men into these
stones. The witch then turned herself into an
elder tree which entwined the 'King Stone'
for many years.

It is claimed that the stones can never be
counted twice and the number made to tally.
In the past, pieces of the 'King Stone' were
chipped off and used as good-luck charms
against the Devil, and by soldiers going
into battle.

Netley Abbey

Founded in 1239 by the Bishop
of Winchester and Henry III, Netley
Abbey is set in a beautiful wooded
valley near Southampton Water.
The romantic ruin was sold to a
builder called Walter Taylor in the
early 18th century, who intended
to take it apart and use the stone
for other building purposes. He
dreamt that a keystone from an
archway fell on him, but thought
nothing of it. Soon after work
began, however, the operation was
forced to stop, after a falling stone
from a window arch killed Taylor.
The site, for me, was a place of
peace and serenity, and I found it
hard to imagine that other visitors
have found a certain unnerving
atmosphere here, highlighted
by sudden temperature drops
and cold spots.
The ruins are said to be haunted
by 'blind Peter', who has been
sighted around the sacristy.

Battle Abbey

The abbey was founded by William the Conqueror, as a thanksgiving for his victory of 1066, and to atone for the terrible loss of life suffered at the Battle of Hastings. The high altar was sited on the spot where King Harold had fallen, and his ghost is said to haunt the abbey ruins.

I visited the abbey on a cold October morning and found it a place of great tranquillity and calm. It was difficult to imagine that, on another cold October morning over 900 years ago, 14,000 men engaged in the slaughter at the Battle of Hastings.

The battlefield site, situated on the hillside to the south of the abbey, is said to run red with blood when the rain falls. A number of ghosts have also been seen, ranging from phantom monks and spectral knights, to red and grey ladies, and one particular ghostly knight seen riding across the battlefield on the anniversary of the conflict.

Bayham Abbey

The romantic ruins of Bayham Abbey are
situated in a picturesque valley. The abbey was
built in the 13th century by Premonstratensian
monks, who, because of the colour of their
robes, were known as 'white canons'.
I found this site to be one of the most tranquil
places I have ever visited. It was almost like
going back in time, and an overwhelming
feeling of quiet and serenity exuded
the whole area.
The hauntings connected with Bayham Abbey
concern phantom monks, who, at midnight on
moonlit nights, have been seen in procession,
noiselessly winding their way through what
remains of the abbey. The sound of chanting
and distant bells have also been heard and some
visitors have reported the smell of burning
incense coming from amongst the ruins.

Minster Lovell Hall

The imposing ruins of this 15th-century manor house stand beside the river Windrush in Oxfordshire. Almost hidden behind the church, Minster Lovell Hall has a history of disappearances, suffering and tragedy.

The hall is reputedly haunted by the ghost of Francis Lovell, who backed the pretender, Lambert Simnel, in 1487. When the rebellion was crushed, Francis fled to Minster Lovell with a price on his head. He hid in an underground room and was looked after by an old servant, the only person to know his whereabouts. When the servant died suddenly Lovell was trapped, and wasn't discovered until 1708, when builders renovating the hall discovered him still seated at a table, with the bones of his dog at his feet.

Another story attached to Minster Lovell begins one Christmas, when William Lovell celebrated his wedding at the hall with his young bride. During a game of hide-and-seek the bride offered to hide. The guests and William searched for weeks, but she was never found, and William eventually died of a broken heart.

Years later, servants found an old oak chest hidden in the attic and inside was a skeleton dressed in a bridal gown. It is thought that the lid had fallen and locked her inside. On windy nights the anguished cries of William can be heard, as he searches for his missing bride.

Richborough Castle

Dating back to AD 43, Richborough Fort was an important part of the Roman coastal defences of Britain, which is difficult to imagine now since the sea is now several miles away. In the 6th and 7th centuries, after the Romans had left, the fort was adapted as an early church.

The still massive walls of Richborough are full of foreboding and the sense of military precision is apparent after all these years. Unsurprisingly, the reputed ghosts who haunt the ruins of Richborourgh are Roman legionaries. They have been seen by many people in and around the fort, still seemingly on duty after so many centuries.

Pevensey Castle

Originally constructed by the Romans in the 4th century, Pevensey Castle has proudly stood the test of time. The impressive ruins now lie about a mile inland, and it's hard to imagine a time when the sea reached right up to the south wall. This was also where William the Conqueror landed his invading army in 1066.

On a cold but bright day I visited Pevensey Castle, and the wind swirled all around, giving the ruins a forlorn feel. The dungeon was flooded after the previous night's heavy rain, but it failed to drown the overwhelming feeling of unease I experienced upon entering the claustrophobic cell.

The 'pale lady of Pevensey', who has been seen by many people stalking the top of the outer walls at dusk, is thought to be the ghost of Lady Pelham, the wife of Sir John Pelham, an early owner of the castle. Lady Pelham held the castle for Sir John while it was beseiged by Richard II at the time of Henry IV's usurpation. The sounds of a spectral battle have also been heard in the vicinity of the castle.

LEFT *Pevensey Castle*

Bramber Castle

Bramber Castle was established in the 11th century by William
de Braoise and, except for a brief period of confiscation, remained
with the family until they died out in 1324.

In late autumn the scant ruins have an air of desolation and decay
about them, and the gloomy ambience does not encourage a long stay.

The hauntings associated with the castle are of a morbid nature.
King John, having fallen out with de Braoise, had him and his wife and
children imprisoned at Windsor and starved to death. The pathetic ghosts
of the children now haunt the ruins of Bramber, usually in the month
of December. They have been seen holding out their hands, as if asking
for food, but if approached they disappear.

The ghost of Maude of Ditchling has been heard wailing amongst
the ruins, after Lord Hubert de Hurst, Maude's husband, found her
with her lover William de Lindfield and had him bricked up alive
in the dungeon.

Appuldurcombe House

LEFT   Once regarded as the grandest house on the Isle of Wight, Appuldurcombe House is now merely a ruined shell. Built in the early 18th century by Sir Robert Worsley, the house has, over the years, been used as a hotel, a school, a temporary home for the monks of Quarr abbey and a billet for troops in both World Wars.

The ruined shell of Appuldurcombe is reported to be haunted by the ghost of a 'mad monk', who has been seen on many occasions by both local people and visitors.

Portchester Castle

RIGHT   The first fortress was built here by the Romans in the 3rd century. It was continually refortified until the 17th century, when it was abandoned, but enjoyed a brief re-employment during the Napoleonic Wars, when the castle was used to house French prisoners.

The castle is situated at the northern extremity of Portsmouth Harbour, and is an impressive ruin. The lengthening shadows formed by the castle in the late afternoon evoke a poignant atmosphere.

Local legends tell of many ghosts associated with the castle. These range from the nebulous 'something tall and whitish', seen by many people, to the phantom woman bending over a grave by the 12th-century church inside the castle grounds. The figure of a monk, walking along the castle front before disappearing, has been seen by a former custodian.

Waverley Abbey

Founded in 1128, Waverley was the first
Cistercian monastery in England. The ruins
stand in a peaceful meadow beside the River
Wey, and although very little remains of
the once magnificent abbey, what is left
is remarkably impressive.
On a cold and misty morning I visited the ruins,
where everything around me was eerily still,
not a sound to be heard, and the atmosphere
intensely ominous. Within an hour the sun
broke through and a dramatic change occurred,
leaving the site with an ambience of peace
and tranquillity. The transformation was
quite amazing.
The grounds of this sedate ruin are said to
be frequented by a ghostly monk. Local legend
tells that he was hung, drawn and quartered
for a long-forgotten crime, and it is believed
that his sad spectre is hunting for his
missing entrails.

Carisbrooke Castle

The Norman castle at Carisbrooke, on the Isle of Wight, was built on the site of an earlier Roman fort, and is in turn surrounded by Elizabethan defences. Charles I was imprisoned here from 1647 to 1648, trying twice to escape before being taken to London and executed.

The castle is very impressive, with a powerfully imposing feel about it that is difficult to describe in words.

The castle is said to be haunted by several ghosts. A 'grey lady' walking her dog has been seen in the moat, and children playing nearby have reported seeing a 'huge man in a long white gown'. Other visitors have seen a face in the well and a woman walking around the moat was spoken to by a young man in a leather jerkin, who then disappeared before her eyes.

Eynsford Castle

LEFT Eynsford Castle dates back to 1088 and was one of the first stone castles to be built by the Normans. William de Eynsford held the manor as a tenant of the Archbishop of Canterbury, but the Eynsford family died out in 1261. The castle was ransacked during a dispute over possession in 1312 and then fell into ruin.

I have my studio in Eynsford and have visited the castle on many occasions and in all seasons, and I still find the ruins have an absorbing, mysterious atmosphere.

A friend of mine who visited the ruins told me that she found a 'cold spot' in the moat, for which she had no explanation. After speaking to several local people I found she was not the first to experience this. Also, according to local people, the vicinity of the castle ruins is rumoured to be haunted by a 'white lady', whose identity is unknown.

Reculver Towers and Roman Fort

RIGHT Standing in a country park, overlooking the sea, are the dramatic twin towers of Reculver. Built on the site of a Roman fort, Reculver was part of the same defensive chain as Richborough Castle. Only half of the fort remains, the rest having crumbled into the sea.

It is said that the ruins have long been haunted by the sounds of a baby crying, which has led to speculation that the Romans buried a live baby here, as part of a sacrifice when building the fort. During excavations some years ago, eleven skeletons of babies were discovered at the ruins.

Farnham Castle Keep

The first castle at Farnham was built around 1138 by Henry de Blois, King Stephen's brother, who was slighted when he fled into exile on Henry II's accession. There are very few records of the castle in the late 12th and early 13th centuries, but it was during this time that the present keep was constructed.

Dominating the town from its hilltop site, Farnham Castle Keep is a sombre ruin. It has a bleak and austere feel to it, making it seem stark and depressing, yet at the same time, and with no obvious explanation, it is also compelling and mysterious – not unlike the unusual haunting attached to it. Many visitors have reported an unidentified and indistinct form haunting the ruins of the keep, and some people have been absolutely terrified by it. Occasionally witnesses have stated that the form resembled a stern-faced woman in a light-coloured gown.

Rycote Chapel

Rycote Chapel was built in 1449 by Richard Quatremayne, and the building remains in good condition today. The interior of the chapel has fine, 17th-century fittings.
The chapel lies at the end of a short drive, almost concealed by trees, as if trying to hide itself in this sleepy corner of Oxfordshire, where time seems to stand still.
There are at least five ghosts reputed to haunt Rycote. A 'grey lady' has been seen both inside the chapel and in the grounds, and a brown-robed monk has also been seen in the vicinity. The Earl of Leicester, who supposedly murdered his wife, is condemned to haunt the chapel, as are Sir Thomas More and Giles Heron, his son-in-law, who were executed together for high treason by Henry VIII.

THE SOUTH WEST

THE SOUTH WEST of England is an area that is rich in myths and legends, from ancient stories that have been handed down through the generations, to more recent manifestations. It is a land of contrasts, boasting a rugged coastline and bleak moors that are home to Tintagel Castle as well as the more gentle landscapes around Stonehenge and Avebury Stone Circle.

This area has a well-known history of association with Druids and at sunrise on Midsummer's Day a spectral Druid priest has been seen entering the long barrow at West Kennet, while at the ancient stone circle in Avebury ghostly figures play amongst the stones on nights lit by a full moon.

More modern hauntings include reported sightings of the infamous Judge Jeffreys at Lydford Castle and ghostly visits by Sir Walter Raleigh to Sherborne Old Castle, minus his head!

LEFT *Okehampton Castle*

Okehampton Castle

Just off the northern edge of Dartmoor, on a hilltop in wooded countryside, stands the ruin of Okehampton Castle. Its shattered walls, silhouetted against the sky, are a permanent reminder of its former glory.

Although impressive, the ruins have a forlorn sadness about them, which made me feel almost as if I were intruding, just by being there.

The castle is said to be haunted by the spectre of Lady Howard. According to legend, every night at midnight the ghost of Lady Howard travels from Okehampton to her old home in Tavistock, in a macabre coach made from the bones of her four husbands. The coach is driven by a headless coachman, and a skeletal hound follows behind. Some believe that she has an eternal task, to remove all the grass from around the castle, but by taking only one blade at a time. A black dog is also reputed to haunt the ruin, and it is said that a glance from the dog will lead to certain death within the year.

Greyfriars, Gloucester

The Grey Friars of the Franciscan order first founded their
friary in Gloucester around 1230, but the current ruins date
from the late 15th and early 16th centuries.
A narrow alleyway at the back of a shopping centre leads to
the ruined fragments of the Franciscan church. Part of the
remains have been incorporated into the modern music
library building. However, the scant ruins remain a pleasure
to visit, and despite being surrounded by modern buildings,
they manage to retain their serene atmosphere.
I was not surprised to learn that the old friary is said to have
a ghost. The mischievous phantom has been active in the part
of the friary now housing the music library. People have
reported hearing banging and crashing sounds coming from
an upstairs room and, upon entering, have found that things
have been moved about but never damaged.

Stonehenge

The magnificent stone circle of Stonehenge is over 5,000 years old, and its
purpose and means of construction remain a mystery to this day. The stones were
once believed to have healing properties and stone scrapings soaked in water
were used by local people to treat wounds.

At different times of the day, and in all seasons, the stones have an intensely
magical presence about them, and always manage to send a chill of excitement
down the spine of the first-time visitor.

There are many legends that abound here. Even today, some believe that the stone
circle was used as a Druid temple, although it dates from an earlier period than the
historical Druids, and there is also a legend that Stonehenge was built by the Devil.
A medieval tale recounted how the stones were flown from Ireland by Merlin.

The true purpose of Stonehenge is still unknown, because the stones
resolutely refuse to give up their secrets.

Avebury Stone Circle

The building of the village of Avebury within the
confines of this mysterious, Neolithic stone
circle, adds – through the juxtaposition of
the ancient pagan past with more recent
history – a sharp sense of continuity
between past and present.

The wind and rain gave Avebury an ominous
feel when I visited the stones, but with a sudden
break in the clouds, the sun shone through and
the sense of foreboding dissolved.

Small, ghostly figures have been seen playing
amongst the stones on nights with a full moon,
and strange lights and music have been heard
as well. Some locals believe this could be the
ghostly return of the annual fair which was
held here until Victorian times.

Farleigh Hungerford Castle

The castle was built in two phases, the first between 1370 and 1380 by Sir Thomas Hungerford, and it remained in Hungerford hands until 1686, with the exception of a brief period of forfeiture during the Wars of the Roses. After that the Hungerfords were forced to sell, and the castle fell into ruins. The impressive ruin still manages to maintain its atmosphere, and the white doves which nest in the towers only add to the feeling of desolation and human abandonment.

Legend tells that the ruins are haunted by the ghost of Lady Agnes Hungerford, who murdered her first husband to marry Sir Edward Hungerford. After his death, however, she and her two accomplices were tried, found guilty of the murder and hanged at Tyburn. Her ghost has been seen in the vicinity of the chapel, next to the crypt.

Tintagel Castle

Although Tintagel Castle is famous for being the birthplace of King Arthur, the current ruins date back to the 13th century, having been built on the site of an earlier fortification. Archaeologists have, however, recently uncovered artefacts dating back to the 6th century, giving substance to the legendary link with King Arthur.

The ruins are set against the spectacular backdrop of the wild and windswept Cornish coast. Sea erosion and land slippage have separated part of the site almost into an island, connected to the headland by some very steep steps. The castle also exudes a mystic atmosphere which has to be experienced first hand.

Local legends report that once or twice a year the extensive ruins disappear and briefly reappear, with the castle complete and in all its former glory, before returning to its present condition.

Blackfriars, Gloucester

This dominican foundation was named after the order's more common name, the Black Friars, a title which refers to the colour of their cloaks, and most of the 13th-century priory church still remains. It is situated in the centre of Gloucester and is only a short distance from the Greyfriars ruins. Access is restricted, but an excellent view is still obtainable from the outside.

Workmen carrying out repairs have reported seeing the ghost of a monk inside the friary, and some have witnessed a friar, with blood pouring from a head wound, running from the nave. Reports in the local newspaper have even told of doors mysteriously locking themselves after people have passed through them.

Lydford Castle

Situated on the western edge of Dartmoor, the castle was described, during the reign of Henry VIII, as 'one of the most heinous, contagious and detestable places within the realm'.
It was a cold winter morning when I visited the grim ruins of the castle, and imagining the site when it was used as a prison, up until the 19th century, was enough to send a shiver down my spine.
The castle is said to be home to the ghost of the infamous Judge Jeffreys, who is doomed to haunt the ruins in the shape of a black pig. A spectral black hound also haunts the area around the castle. This is said to be the spirit of the wicked Lady Howard, who also haunts Okehampton Castle.

Old Wardour Castle

Built by Lord Lovel in the late 14th century, Old Wardour Castle saw most of its action during the Civil War. It was first besieged by 1,300 Roundheads in May 1643, when the castle held out for five days manned only by Lady Blanche Arundell and a handful of retainers. By March the following year the castle had been retaken after a four-month siege by Lord Arundell, but unfortunately the castle had been so heavily damaged that it was never repaired.

This romantic ruin has an unusual, shattered hexagonal keep. It is situated on the edge of a lake, surrounded by landscaped grounds complete with a rockwork grotto.

An eerie belief associated with Old Wardour was that white owls were the harbingers of death to the head of the Arundell household, and the ghost of Lady Blanche Arundell has been seen around the walls of the ruins as dusk falls.

West Kennet Long Barrow

The Neolithic tomb of West Kennet is one of Britain's finest examples of a chambered long barrow. It lies on the crest of a hill, overlooking Silbury Hill and Avebury. Artefacts found in the tomb indicate that it was in use for over 1,000 years before being sealed off.

The long barrow can be found at the end of a brisk, uphill walk from the road, and the burial chamber can be overwhelmingly claustrophobic.

The ghost of a Druid priest is said to haunt the long barrow. He has been seen entering the tomb at sunrise on Midsummer's Day, usually followed by a phantom white dog.

Sherborne Old Castle

Built in the early 12th century by Roger de Caen, Bishop of Salisbury, Sherborne Old Castle was a strongly defended, but palatial, retreat for the Bishops of Salisbury, commanding an important junction of the London-Exeter road. Legend has it that the castle had a curse placed on it to prevent it leaving church hands. The Earl of Somerset and Sir Walter Raleigh were both executed while in possession of the castle.

Enough remains of the castle to allow the imagination to visualize its former splendour.

The ghost of Sir Walter Raleigh is said to haunt the old castle. His headless phantom has been seen wandering the grounds on Michaelmas Eve (29th September).

RIGHT *Sherborne Old Castle*

Berry Pomeroy Castle

The late medieval castle of Berry Pomeroy
is now only a romantic ruin, but it has often
been referred to as one of the most haunted
castles in England.

When I visited the castle, early in the season,
there were no other visitors, and after only a
short time wandering amongst the ruins,
I felt that I had absorbed the forlorn atmosphere
of the place.

The castle ruins are said to be haunted by
ghosts from the de Pomeroy family, who held
the castle for 500 years. The most famous is the
'white lady', thought to be Margaret de
Pomeroy, who was imprisoned and starved to
death by her sister Eleanor, in what is now
known as Margaret's Tower. The 'blue lady',
whose appearance is said to herald the death
of a castle resident, is not so easily identified. It
is generally agreed, however, that she was a
de Pomeroy girl who murdered her baby after
being made pregnant by her father.
Visitors have also reported hearing the ghostly
sounds of a baby crying, of footsteps and of the
slamming of non-existent doors.

Hailes Abbey

Founded in the 13th century for the Cistercian order, Hailes Abbey was once a great
centre of pilgrimage in England. This was because the abbey possessed a holy relic –
a phial containing Christ's blood – which, however, was later revealed as a fake.
When I visited the abbey it was late afternoon, and the shadows were starting to grow longer,
giving the ruins a sinister feel. It was not hard to imagine that people, over the years, have
reported being overwhelmed by a feeling of sudden fear when visiting the abbey.
Spectral monks have been seen wandering amongst the ruins by local people who
now avoid the area after dark.

THE EAST

THE EASTERN REGION OF England is no stranger to ghost stories. In the early morning light, when the mist rolls off the water and across the even land, it is not difficult to believe that this is an area famed for its myths and legends.

The diverse tales that are told in this chapter bring to life some of the more fascinating events In the region's history. In this eerie landscape people tell of terrifying hauntings that range from the hysterical screams of 'The She-wolf of France' at Castle Rising Castle, to the fiddler of Binham Priory who vanished into a secret underground passage and was never seen or heard of again.

LEFT *Hadleigh Castle*

Hadleigh castle

Originally built in the 13th century by Hugh de Burgh, and later rebuilt by Edward III, Hadleigh Castle looks out over the Essex marshes and the Thames estuary. The castle ruins were immortalized by John Constable in his paintings and sketches.

The ruins are bleak, and the cries of sea birds overhead convey a feeling of melancholy among the scant remains.

The vicinity of the castle has several reputed ghosts, although some of these can be attributed to smugglers. In the 18th century, smugglers were known to burn coloured lights in the ruins to frighten off superstitious locals, who believed the castle to be haunted by evil spirits. The ghost of a woman in white was once seen by a local girl and a 'filmy human shape' was seen at night by a group of youngsters in the 1920s.

Binham Priory

The Benedictine priory of Binham was founded in the 11th century and the original nave, set amongst the extensive ruins, is used today as the parish church.

Legend tells of a secret underground passage that ran to Walsingham, over three miles away, and a mysterious 'black monk' who, on moonless nights, haunted the route of the tunnel from above ground. One day a fiddler, accompanied by his dog, entered the tunnel playing his fiddle, while the local people followed above ground, listening to his music. At a place later known as 'fiddler's hill', the music stopped, and although the dog reappeared, shivering with terror, the fiddler was never seen or heard of again.

Castle Rising Castle

The mid 12th-century ruin of Castle Rising Castle, set within massive defensive earthworks, was the home and prison of Isabella, Queen Dowager of England, also known as the 'she-wolf of France'. The fine summer day had turned cloudy when I visited Castle Rising, which dramatically changed the ambience within the massive keep. The many passages and corridors became darker and more ominous as the natural light faded. According to legend, the ghost of Isabella haunts the upper levels of the ruined keep. Her 27-year imprisonment ended in madness and many visitors have reported hearing her shrieks of hysteria around the castle.

Burgh Castle

Known today as Burgh Castle, this site was actually built as the Roman fort of Gariannonum, in the late 3rd century, and was originally part of the Saxon Shore defences. Although the receding waters of the sea have left the castle behind, and the sea wall is long gone, the remaining walls are still a formidable sight.

I found the massive, flint-faced walls, with their leaning and fallen bastions awe-inspiring, and could see why many people at the time thought the place had been built by giants.

Legend tells us that every year on 3rd July, a ghostly figure wrapped in a white banner plunges from the top of the ramparts, only to disappear once it has hit the ground, and that in the early morning mists of May, the castle has been seen complete and in all its former glory, before returning to its present, ruinous state.

Thetford Warren Lodge

In the 12th century the lodge was built for
the warrener, who looked after the production of
rabbits, a valued source of meat for the royal
table. In later years it was used as a lazar house
or leper hospital.
The lodge can be found in a pleasant clearing in
the woods, and although it is a small site, it is
still well worth a visit, but not after dark!
A phantom leper is believed to haunt the
lodge. With a ravaged face and burning eyes,
he has been sighted both at the ruin and
wandering around the area of the lodge,
gibbering insensibly.

THE MIDLANDS

THE MIDLAND AREA IS the very 'heart of England'. It is an area rich in tales of the supernatural, many of them connected with the spectacular castles, abbeys, manors, halls and standing stones under the protective wing of English Heritage.

Wingfield Manor is reputedly haunted by the ghost of Mary, Queen of Scots and Arbor Low Stone Circle is avoided by local people after dark for fear of encountering a 'boggart'.

A mysterious man in black, who some believe to be the devil himself, has been seen standing outside the Nine Ladies Stone Circle and a disembodied arm has been observed at Sutton Scarsdale Hall, beckoning witnesses towards the cellar area.

The ghosts of two young lovers killed during the Civil War while trying to escape a siege preside at Goodrich Castle, and Haughmond Abbey is home to a spectral monk who wanders amongst the ruins.

LEFT *Peveril Castle*

Peveril Castle

Set on a hilltop high above the picturesque village of Castleton is the majestic ruin of Peveril Castle. Known as the 'castle of the peak', the views from the ruins are breathtaking.

The castle was built in the late 11th century by William Peveril, an illegitimate son of William the Conqueror, and is mentioned in the Domesday Book of 1086. By the 15th century, the castle was abandoned, and left to fall into ruin.

To reach the castle I took the long winding path from the village, with the wind howling all around and the clouds overhead moving at a rapid pace. By the time I reached the ruin it had started to rain, and the site was engulfed by an eerie and chilling atmosphere.

The ghost of a 'white knight' has been seen standing near the ramparts, while a phantom dog and horse have also been observed in the area near the ruined keep. Strange noises, including the sound of a lady singing, have been heard emanating from the ruins.

Gainsborough Old Hall

Early written records tell us that parts of Gainsborough Old Hall were built between 1465 and 1480 on the site of an earlier castle. The medieval manor house is one of the most complete to survive in the country today. Surrounded as it is by modern houses, the Old Hall is something of a surprise. The beautiful architecture, combined with the amazing restoration work that has been carried out, allows visitors to experience the hall as if they have stepped back in time.

The hall claims to have at least two ghosts, the first dating back to when the original castle stood on the site. Legend tells us that King Sweyne of Denmark was killed here in 1014, whilst attacking the castle during the second Danish invasion of England. His ghostly moans and groans have been heard echoing throughout the hall. The second apparition is that of a 'grey lady', thought to be the daughter of a former owner. She was seen by a caretaker disappearing through a wall and later renovations revealed a secret doorway at the exact spot where she had disappeared.

Wingfield Manor

Built in the mid 15th century, the romantic ruin of Wingfield Manor was once a prison for Mary, Queen of Scots. The mansion was partly demolished during the Civil War and abandoned in the 1770s.

I had to walk up a muddy track to reach the magnificent ruins and found them to be well worth the trek. The dark sandstone adds to the eerie atmosphere of this Gothic manor and it is not surprising that people have seen things here for which they have no explanation.

The most famous ghost associated with Wingfield is that of Mary, Queen of Scots. Legend recalls that she revisits the manor's ballroom on certain nights of the year.

Workmen carrying out repairs have seen 'phantom lights' in unoccupied areas of the ruins and several visitors have reported seeing an 'unusual bluish light of indefinite shape' in the undercroft.

Arbor Low Stone Circle

Known locally as the 'Stonehenge of
Derbyshire', Arbor Low Stone Circle occupies
an open field over 1,000 feet above sea level.
It is thought that Neolithic people used the circle
as a temple for sun worship, and that the stones,
although now lying flat, once stood erect.
On a cold autumn morning I visited Arbor Low,
where the overwhelming feeling of desolation
and seclusion which possessed me was only
intensified by the sharp wind blowing in
gusts all around me.
Local people are known to avoid the area
after dark for fear of encountering a 'boggart',
the regional 'vengeful spirit' of legend. Ghostly
sightings have been reported for centuries and
local legend states that anyone who spends the
night within the stone circle will awaken
the spirits of the dead.

Nine Ladies Stone Circle

Situated above Darley Dale, on Stanton Moor, is the
Nine Ladies Stone Circle. The circle was originally part of an early
Bronze Age burial site, and to this day locals have been known to
avoid the area after dark, fearing the spirits of the dead.
The legend of the stones is a well-known tale of nine ladies, turned
to stone for the crime of dancing on the Sabbath to the music
of a fiddle played by the Devil himself.
The figure of a man dressed all in black, standing just outside
the stone circle, has often been seen, but his identity remains a mystery.
Some say he is the Devil, checking on his handiwork.

Bolsover Castle

Built on a wooded ridge, Bolsover Castle dominates the surrounding landscape. Very little remains of the original castle, which was built in the 12th century by William Peveril. It fell into disrepair in 1216, after it was besieged by King John, and in the 17th century it was mostly demolished by Charles Cavendish, who built the present castle in its place.

From the outside the castle is very impressive. The ghostly experiences recorded include phantom smells and pinches or slaps from unseen hands. A much more interesting sighting, however, is that of the figure of a woman, seen putting a wrapped bundle, thought to be a baby, into the fire in the kitchen.

Moreton Corbet Castle

Medieval ruins, with the remains of a partly-built Elizabethan mansion, are all that is left of Moreton Corbet Castle. It belonged to the Corbet family, who started work on the house in 1606, but work was never completed and the building was damaged by fire during the Civil War.

The magnificent ruin is an eerie place to visit. Inside the castle shell all sounds are amplified, which makes you feel you are not alone.

The ruins are said to be both cursed and haunted. Sir Vincent Corbet fell foul of a Puritan neighbour, Paul Homeyard, during the building of the house, after refusing him aid during the persecutions by King James. Homeyard cursed the property, saying that it would never be finished. Homeyard's ghost returns to haunt the mansion on moonlit nights, when his forlorn figure has been seen wandering the ruins.

Sutton Scarsdale Hall

Built in the early 18th century, on the site of a former house, Sutton Scarsdale Hall was once described as one of the most magnificent houses in Derbyshire. Too modern to be classed as Romantic, this baroque ruin is situated on the opposite side of the valley from Hardwick Old Hall, and is clearly visible from the M1 motorway. The hall is now little more than a shell, and appears lonely and derelict. While wandering around inside, my footsteps sounded much louder than they should have, and an unnerving feeling of desolation pervaded the whole site.

The ghosts said to haunt the ruin are numerous and take on many forms. These include the smell of tobacco, detected in different parts of the hall, hovering coloured lights, which appear for several seconds before disappearing and phantom footsteps heard wandering the ruins. Witnesses have reported seeing a disembodied arm that seems to beckon towards the cellar area, and although there is no explanation for this, it seems likely that some nefarious deed once took place there.

Goodrich Castle

The red sandstone ruins of Goodrich Castle
stand on a hill overlooking the River Wye.
The castle was in use from the 13th century
but was slighted by Cromwell's troops
after a siege in 1646.
Goodrich is remarkably complete and has lots
of nooks and crannies to explore.
The reputed haunting arises from a tragic love
story, and goes back to the siege of 1646.
Alice, the niece of Colonel Birch, a
Parliamentarian, took refuge in the castle with
her lover, Charles Clifford, a Royalist. Birch
besieged the castle and, fearing for their lives,
the couple tried to escape. One moonlit night,
after forcing their way through the
Roundheads, they attempted to cross the river
at the ford. However, they had not allowed for
the heavy rain that had flooded the river and
were swept away to their deaths. Their ghosts
have been seen around the castle walls and by
the river at the foot of the ruins. In stormy
weather it is said that their death shrieks
can be heard coming from the river.

Arthur's Stone

The impressive Arthur's Stone is a fine example of a Neolithic burial chamber, where the huge capstone is supported on nine uprights. Legend has it that this is the burial place of a giant killed by King Arthur on this very spot.

The hollows found in the nearby Quoit Stone are said to be marks made by King Arthur's knees, where he knelt to pray after the giant's demise.

Situated in the borderland between England and Wales, Arthur's Stone has a magical presence about it when visited at first light when the almost total silence of the surrounding countryside evokes an enchanted atmosphere.

Haughmond Abbey

Haughmond Abbey was founded c. 1130 for the Augustinian order. Legend has it that it was linked to Holy Cross Abbey and High Ercall by underground passages that extended for over three miles to each location.

It was a cloudy summer day when I visited the ruins and the whole place had a feeling of peacefulness about it. When I asked the custodian about the reported sightings of ghostly monks, she told me that, although she hadn't seen anything herself, a previous custodian had seen a spectral monk wandering amongst the ruins. Over the years, many visitors to the abbey have also reported seeing the monk.

LEFT *Haughmond Abbey*

Croxden Abbey

Croxden was a Cistercian abbey, founded
in 1176 and finally completed in 1254. It
was abandoned during the dissolution of the
monasteries and from that point the
building began to deteriorate.
The sun shone through the trees when I visited
the abbey, and the tranquil atmosphere was
enlivened by tales of ghostly figures wandering
around the ruins. Many people have, over the
years, reported seeing phantom monks and
nuns amongst the ruins, the sightings frequently
occurring on warm summer nights.

Rufford Abbey

LEFT Rufford Abbey was built in 1148 for the Cistercian order. After the dissolution of the monasteries it was granted to the 6th Earl of Shrewsbury, who pulled down most of the abbey and built an Elizabethan mansion on the site.
Today, the ruins of both abbey and mansion can be found in a country park. The undercroft of the abbey has been restored but still retains an enigmatic atmosphere of mystery. There have been many reported hauntings associated with Rufford, the most infamous of which is that of a giant monk with a grinning skull beneath his black cowl. He has been seen descending a staircase and wandering the grounds which surround the ruins. It is even been reported that his appearance caused the demise of a local man, who was literally scared to death!

Rushton Triangular Lodge

RIGHT Completed by Sir Thomas Tresham in 1597, the lodge symbolizes the Holy Trinity and the Mass, with three walls with three windows, with three gables to each, three storeys and a three-sided chimney.
Legend tells that the lodge is haunted by a gypsy fiddler, whose phantom fiddle has been heard coming from the lodge. Lord Cullen, the then owner, offered fifty pounds to anyone who would explore the secret underground passage that had recently been discovered. The gypsy fiddler took up the offer and entered the tunnel playing his fiddle. After a short time the music stopped and the tunnel was found to have collapsed. The fiddler was never seen again and the tunnel was bricked up.

Lilleshall Abbey

The abbey was originally founded in 1148 for the Arrouaisian order, but later became Augustinian. More of the abbey would survive today but for its conversion into a fortified stronghold during the Civil War.

As if hiding from the modern world, the abbey ruins can be found tucked away at the edge of a wood, by a stream. The extensive ruins are surrounded by ancient yew trees which help the visitor to recapture the abbey's past magnificence.

Over the years many visitors have heard strange noises coming from the ruins in the early evening. It is said that they sound like the moans and shrieks of someone being tortured. A previous custodian was reported as having seen the black-robed figure of an elderly Augustinian monk, who spoke to him before disappearing, and ghostly footsteps have been heard around the ruins late at night.

YORKSHIRE & HUMBERSIDE

YORKSHIRE AND HUMBERSIDE IS an impressive region both for heritage and hauntings. The rugged countryside and spectacular coastline has inspired countless ghostly, mysterious tales, including Whitby Abbey's famous connection with Bram Stoker's *Dracula*. It is no surprise that this wonderfully evocative landcsape is reportedly the home of so many spectral visits.

As well as traditional ghostly manifestations, this region boasts some more unusual sightings. Clifford's Tower in York experiences a rare sight, thought to be connected to the mass suicide and massacre of Jews who fled there for safety in the 12th century, while Spotforth Castle boasts an almost unique apparition featuring just the top half of a woman.

LEFT *Rievaulx Abbey*

Rievaulx Abbey

The abbey of Rievaulx was founded in 1132 and became the first Cistercian abbey in the north of England. In 1322, Edward II stayed at Rievaulx and was caught unprepared by the Scots, and defeated at the Battle of Byland. He fled to York, leaving the abbey at the mercy of the marauding invaders.

Tucked away in the picturesque Rye valley, the abbey can be found at the bottom of a steep hill. The setting and the ruins are truly magnificent, and it is easy to visualize what it must have looked like in its prime.

In the still and hushed environment, some people have heard the unmistakable sound of ghostly ringing bells, while others have reported a feeling of sadness overwhelming them while wandering through the ruins. In some cases they have been so distressed that they have had to leave. It has also been reported that a ghostly monk has been seen within the ruins.

Clifford's Tower

The mound that the tower stands on was constructed in 1069–70, but the original wooden keep burned down in 1190. During a time of anti-Jewish rioting, many Jews fled to the tower for safety. Unable to defend themselves many committed mass suicide in the tower. The remainder were massacred by the mob, who eventually stormed the tower after setting it alight.

The present tower was completed in the early 14th century as the keep of York Castle. The name is thought to derive from Roger de Clifford, a Lancastrian leader who was hanged in chains from the walls of the tower in 1322.

Situated in the centre of the city of York, the tower is a simple but impressive structure.

Although a fire in 1648 has reduced it to only a shell, the remains are well worth a visit and still hold a lot of atmosphere, especially early in the morning.

The tower boasts an unusual manifestation. It has been reported over the years that the walls have been seen with blood pouring from them, blood said to be that of the Jews who sought refuge in the tower. In recent years this phenomenon was thought to be caused by iron oxide in the stone, although no other stone from the same quarry contains that mineral.

Spofforth Castle

Spofforth Castle has a
13th-century undercroft, cut into
the rock, but the remainder of the
structure is mostly 15th century.
The castle was dismantled in the
early 17th century.

Spofforth Castle is an odd ruin,
situated on a patch of land within
an urban housing estate. Despite
the number of houses surrounding
the castle, I did not see a soul the
whole time I was there. It felt as if
the entire area was deserted.

The reputed haunting at these
ruins is said to be almost unique.
The apparition is of the top half
of a woman, who appears bluish-
white in colour and throws herself
off the top of the tower. Her
identity is unknown but she has
been seen by many people,
including a group of school
children and their teacher.

Roche Abbey

Founded by the Cistercian order in 1147, Roche Abbey was originally known as the abbey of Santa Maria de Rupe. 'Roche' means 'rock', and legend has it that a vision of the crucifix appeared on a certain rock nearby, and inspired the order to settle there.

The peaceful, tranquil ruins are almost hidden at the bottom of a small valley. The magnificent arches, which still stand intact, dominate the surrounding countryside.

A spectral monk dressed in the white robes of the Cistercian order has been seen by visitors, moving with urgency amongst the ruins, while local people have reported strange and unexplainable noises coming from the surrounding area. The abbey house also has its share of phantoms, with a 'grey lady' sighted at one of the upstairs windows. The cries of a ghostly baby have also been reported, along with the sounds of heavy footsteps on an empty staircase.

Skipsea Castle

The original Skipsea Castle was built by Drogo de Bevere, a Flemish soldier of fortune, who was awarded lands by William the Conqueror for services rendered. He was also given the hand in marriage of one of William's nieces. Drogo, however, killed his bride and hid her body, and was forced to flee the country to escape William's fury. The castle was finally destroyed by order of Henry III in 1221, following the revolt of William de Fortibus, and all that remains today are earthworks. The castle mound is accessible at any time via a farmer's field, but the track can be muddy and the going slow and arduous.

Some believe that the ghost of Lady de Bevere haunts the earth ramparts. According to legend she is yearning for someone to discover her bones, so that she can be given a Christian burial. The 'white lady' has been seen by many local people at different times of the day and night.

Byland Abbey

After a few false starts, Byland Abbey was finally established in the late 12th century by the Cistercian order. In its day it was regarded as one of the three great monasteries of the North, along with Rievaulx and Fountains.

Situated in a picturesque valley at the foot of the Hambleton hills, the ruins are almost hidden from the road. When I visited the abbey it rose out of the early-morning mist and seemed almost magical.

Some of the earliest-recorded ghost stories in Britain were written by a monk from Byland, around the year 1400, when he wrote twelve short ghost stories in Latin.

A few years ago, a historical re-enactment group were caught by bad weather and forced to stay overnight in the abbey's museum. One of the members was woken at around 2.30 a.m. by a gentle rocking motion to his body. When he reached out to see what was causing it, he found nothing. It was thought that the movement came from the ghost of a monk, waking him for the first prayers of the day. Matins were said at 2.30 every morning and, because of the vow of silence, one of the monks would wake the others by gently rocking them out of their sleep.

Whitby Abbey

High above the town, overlooking the harbour,
stands the magnificent Gothic ruin of Whitby
Abbey. The abbey was originally founded in 657
by St Hilda, and was rebuilt in the late 1070s,
after being destroyed by Viking invaders.
The novelist Bram Stoker immortalized the
abbey by setting scenes from his book *Dracula*
amongst the ruins.
Legend has it that the abbey has several ghosts,
including St Hilda, who has been seen in some
of the upper empty windows, wearing a white
shroud. A nun who broke her vows is said to
haunt the stairs to the dungeon, where she was
bricked up alive, and at dawn on the old
Christmas Day (6th January) faint echoes of
a ghostly choir have been heard coming
from the ruins.

LEFT & ABOVE *Whitby Abbey*

Conisbrough Castle

Nothing substantial is known of the original castle, except that it was built by William de Warenne after the Norman Conquest. The current castle was built around 1180 by Hamelin Plantagenet, Henry II's half-brother, and the magnificent keep is one of the finest examples of its kind in Europe. Apart from a short siege, the castle's later history is somewhat uneventful and by 1538 it had fallen into ruin.

The ruin of Conisbrough Castle is a surprising site. I arrived just as the castle was closing, and the custodian said I could accompany him as he locked up. The awesome keep was even more impressive up close than it had been from a distance, to the extent of making the rest of the ruin pale in comparison.

Numerous ghosts have been reported here over the years, including that of a 'grey monk', seen wandering the grounds. An unknown 'white lady' has been seen at the top of the keep, where she was rumoured to have been pushed to her death. Mysterious lights have been sighted in the vicinity of the chapel, and phantom footsteps have also been heard in the great keep.

Richmond Castle

Built by Alan 'the red' of Brittany, one of
William the Conqueror's most loyal supporters,
Richmond was one of the country's earliest
stone castles. Thankfully, the castle has never
really fallen into total neglect, and was returned
to use by the military during both World Wars.
The impressive keep at Richmond still stands to
its original height and, although the castle
played no significant role in history, it still has
its share of secrets.

Legends tell of a secret underground passage
that leads to the nearby Easby Abbey, and of
the ghostly drummer boy whose drum beats are
still heard long after he had disappeared without
trace in the hidden tunnels. Other legends
propose that King Arthur and his knights lie
sleeping under the ruins in a secret cavern,
waiting for the day when they will return.

Thornton Abbey

Founded as a priory in 1139 for the Augustinian canons, Thornton was elevated to abbey status in 1148, after it became wealthy and influential. The magnificent gatehouse is said to be one of the finest examples of such a structure in the United Kingdom.

The remote setting of the abbey adds to the overall ambience, and even on a warm sunny day the ruins retain an eerie and unnerving presence. The stone gargoyles seemed to watch me wherever I went, filling me with cautious apprehension.

The ruins are believed to be haunted by the spectre of the 14th abbot of Thornton, Thomas de Gretham, who was accused of witchcraft and dabbling in the black arts. For his crimes and sins against God he was bricked up alive in a dungeon. His remains were discovered centuries later by workmen, who found his skeleton sitting at a table, with a candlestick and book at his side.

Pickering Castle

The first castle at Pickering was built by William the Conqueror in the years after the Norman Conquest, and was a simple earth-and-timber construction. In subsequent years it was rebuilt in stone and extended. The castle played no part in the Civil War and by that time was already falling into ruin.

Some guidebooks have described Pickering as unexciting, even ordinary, but I discovered it was full of atmosphere, and even heard unexplained footsteps in the Diate Hill Tower. The custodian was unable to shed any light on this and categorically denied believing in ghosts, but he did mention that he didn't hang around after dark!

A previous custodian, in the 1950s, saw the ghost of a tall monk, dressed in a long grey robe, move across the grounds towards the ruined keep. His face was covered by his hood and his hands were outstretched as if he was carrying something unseen.

Scarborough Castle

High on the cliffs, dominating the town and harbour below, are the magnificent ruins of Scarborough Castle. Built on the site of a Roman signal station, the present castle dates from the 12th century and even after being severely damaged during the Civil War, it continued in service, as a prison and then a barracks, until the end of World War I. Enough remains of the castle to show how impressive it must once have been, and when the wind howls in from the North Sea, and the clouds overhead race across the sky, the proud castle still commands a striking presence. Piers Gaveston, Edward II's favourite, was captured here in 1312 and taken to Warwick for execution, but it is rumoured that his ghost returns here, to haunt the ruins of the castle. The headless apparition of Gaveston is said to lure people over the battlements to their deaths.

THE
NORTH

THE NORTH OF ENGLAND boasts a beautiful, but sometimes bleak and forbidding landscape, and is the site of many reported hauntings. The area's diverse, and often violent, history is well-documented by its tales of ghostly manifestations.

The location of the region has made it the target of many invasions through the centuries and spectral sightings include the ghost of Prior Olaf, a Viking invader at Tynemouth Priory, while Bowes Castle is said to house the ghosts of Romans murdered during the final days of the Roman occupation.

Dunstanburgh Castle has an even more disturbing story to tell. The Earl of Lancaster was the victim of an inept executioner who took eleven blows to remove his head. Reports claim that he can still be seen around the castle carrying his mangled head.

LEFT *Tynemouth Priory*

Tynemouth Priory

The original early Christian monastery was founded in the 7th century, but later destroyed by Danish invaders in the 9th century. It was refounded by the Benedictine order in 1090. Already surrounded by a curtain wall with defensive towers, the priory received licence to crenellate in 1296, thus becoming a priory within a castle. After the dissolution of the monasteries the priory underwent military occupation and was even in use as a coastal battery during World War II.

Situated on a headland at the entrance to the Tyne estuary, the windswept ruins are bleak and desolate.

Legend has it that the ruins are haunted by Olaf, a Viking, who was wounded during a raid and tended by the monks. He joined the order and rose to become prior. Olaf's brother was killed during another Viking raid on the priory and it is said that Olaf died of grief while praying in the chapel. His ghost has been seen many times, standing by the ruined walls looking out to sea, usually during daylight hours on fine days when the wind is blowing in from the east.

Bowes Castle

Bowes Castle was built on the site of a former Roman fort in the 12th century, and served as one of Henry II's great tower keeps. I arrived at the castle at the same time as the rain, and took cover in the ruins to avoid getting wet. As the rainfall increased, the sky grew darker, and inside the ruins it seemed as if night had fallen. The atmosphere took on an uncomfortably unwelcoming feel, and just as I was about to suffer the wet in preference to lingering in the tower, the sun broke through and the spell was broken.

Bowes is not haunted by a single ghost but by an entire squad. During the final days of the Roman occupation of Britain, the garrison at Bowes ran amok and stole anything of any value, mainly gold. The angry locals retaliated by attacking the fort and massacring the garrison. Unfortunately for them, however, the gold and treasure had already been hidden and has never since been recovered. It is reputed that on the anniversary of the massacre the ghosts of the murdered men appear and ritually bury the gold and treasure.

Warkworth Castle

The first castle was built in the mid 12th century and every century since has left its mark. Warkworth is one of the most impressive examples of an aristocratic fortified residence in Britain, and its magnificent keep still dominates the village today. The ruins stand above the River Coquet, within a loop which forms a natural moat around them. The ruins are said to be haunted by a 'grey lady', believed to be the ghost of Margaret Neville, wife of the first Earl of Northumberland. Her spectre has been seen by visitors as she walks away from the Grey Mare's Tail Tower. An uncanny presence has also been felt in one of the wine cellars, which was formerly used as an overflow prison, and the ghost of a young man has been seen running along the walls.

Carlisle Castle

Built in 1092 by William Rufus, Carlisle Castle has seen over 800 years of continuous military use. During its eventful history the castle has been home to Andrew Harcla, Earl of Carlisle, who was executed for his alliance with Robert the Bruce, and Mary, Queen of Scots during the early part of her many years of imprisonment. During the Civil War the castle was held for the king, but finally surrendered to the Scots after a lengthy siege. It also fell to the Jacobites in 1745.

Today the castle is home to the headquarters of the King's Own Royal Border Regiment, and is now besieged only by tourists.

It is reputed that the castle is haunted by the ghost of an unknown lady. During renovations her skeleton was found immured in the wall of the keep. She was dressed in silk tartan and had valuable rings on her fingers. A soldier on guard duty once challenged her ghost, but collapsed from shock after she disappeared in front of him.

He died a few hours later.

Dunstanburgh Castle

Built in the 14th century by Thomas, Earl of Lancaster, Dunstanburgh Castle was designed more as a refuge than a fortress. The fortifications were strengthened in the 1380s by John of Gaunt, but the castle eventually surrendered to Edward IV's siege, and then slowly fell into ruin.

At one time Dunstanburgh was the largest castle in Northumberland and the forlorn ruins today echo with a faint cry of its former glory. I found the castle high on a cliff after walking the one and a half miles from Craster, and with the wind howling in off the North Sea it was easy to believe the legends attached to the ruins. One such legend concerns Sir Guy, a wandering knight whose ghost haunts the ruins after failing to release a 'lady in white' from her magical imprisonment there. Another phantom is that of Thomas, Earl of Lancaster, who built the castle. He fell foul of Edward II and was executed by a bungling executioner who took eleven strokes to cut off his head. His tragic ghost has been seen carrying his mangled head, with the face still contorted in its dying agonies. The spectral form of Margaret of Anjou, the wife of Henry VI, has also been seen wandering the ruins.

Lindisfarne Priory

The original priory on the island of Lindisfarne, now known as Holy Island, was founded in 635 and became a place of pilgrimage after the enshrinement of St Cuthbert in 698. The present priory ruins were established in the 12th century by Benedictine monks from Durham, and even after the dissolution of monastic houses, in 1537, Holy Island remained a place of pilgrimage, as it is today. It is worth remembering that a visit to Holy Island can only be made during low tide, when the causeway can be crossed. The whole island has a tranquil feel to it, despite its exposed location on the North Sea coast. The priory ruins have lost none of their magical qualities, even though the ravages of time have taken their toll. It is said by islanders that the ghost of St Cuthbert haunts the ruins of the priory and his apparition has been seen on nights when the moon is full and the tide is rolling across the causeway. A phantom white dog has also been seen amongst the priory ruins.

Castlerigg Stone Circle

The circle was once described by John Keats as 'a dismal cirque of Druid stones upon a forlorn moor'. On a cold, wet autumn morning that may be a fair description, but at other times the stones, which are thought to date back to around 3000 BC, are surrounded by a sense of mystery and intrigue. Wandering amongst the stones for a short while gave me a feeling of peace and contentment. I spent the best part of the morning there and did not want to leave. Local legend states that the stones can never be counted more than once to reveal the same number, and, over the years, mysterious lights have been seen moving around the stones, for which there is no natural explanation.

Hylton Castle

LEFT The ruined shell of a 15th-century gatehouse keep is all that visibly remains of Hylton Castle. The keep was incorporated into an 18th-century mansion and then Gothicized in the 1860s, before being abandoned. Hylton Castle stands in the middle of a modern housing estate, alone in a small landscaped park. In these surroundings it is difficult to imagine the castle's past, but traces of the original atmosphere of this historic site can be felt at sunrise or sunset.

The legend of the 'Cauld Lad', associated with Hylton Castle, has many versions. Some say it is the spirit of a mischievous 'elf' or 'brownie' who haunted the castle in the 15th century by playing tricks on the kitchen staff. Another version is that the ghost of Roger Skelton, a stable boy murdered in the early 17th century by his master, Sir Robert Hylton, haunts the ruin. His body was hidden in a deep pond nearby and his spectre has been seen, dripping wet and with teeth chattering, at the scene of his murder.

Gisborough Priory

RIGHT Founded in 1119 by Robert de Brus for the Augustinian order, the priory was partly destroyed by fire in 1289. Most of the remains are early 14th century, including the magnificent east wall, which still stands to a substantial height.

Legend tells that the ruins are haunted by a monk in a black habit, said to appear on the first new moon of every year to ensure that a stash of hidden treasure has not been disturbed. The treasure also has another guardian, said to be a raven or crow, which will turn into the Devil if the treasure is discovered.

INDEX

ACKNOWLEDGEMENTS

I would like to extend my thanks to all those people who have been involved in the production of this book. A special mention must go to Peter Mills, my long-suffering printer, for producing such wonderful prints of all the photographs. Thanks also to English Heritage for their help and support and to everyone at Collins & Brown.
Finally a hearty 'thank-you' to all the ghosts, ghouls, spectres and phantoms who made this book possible.

Selections of limited edition photographic prints from this book are available for sale. Details can be found on my web site or by writing to me at my studio.

John Mason
The Studio
High Street
Eynsford
Kent DA4 0AA

Email: john@hauntedrealm.com
Web site: www.hauntedrealm.com